Can a Wolf Raise a Cat?

by Mrs. Olson's class
with Tony Stead

capstone

A Wolf

by Aaron, Ella, Heidi, Lili, and Rowan

A wolf is a wild animal.

A wolf howls, has pups, and eats meat.

A wolf is a wild animal.

But a wolf can play.

Wolves

by Ella, Hayden, Kate, Kian, Madi, and Quentin

Wolves have strong jaws and sharp teeth.

They have a leader, and they live in a pack.

Wolves live in a pack.

A Cat

by Aaron, Ella, Hayden, Nora, and Quentin

A cat is a pet.

A cat can climb.

A cat is a pet.

A cat has whiskers and paws.

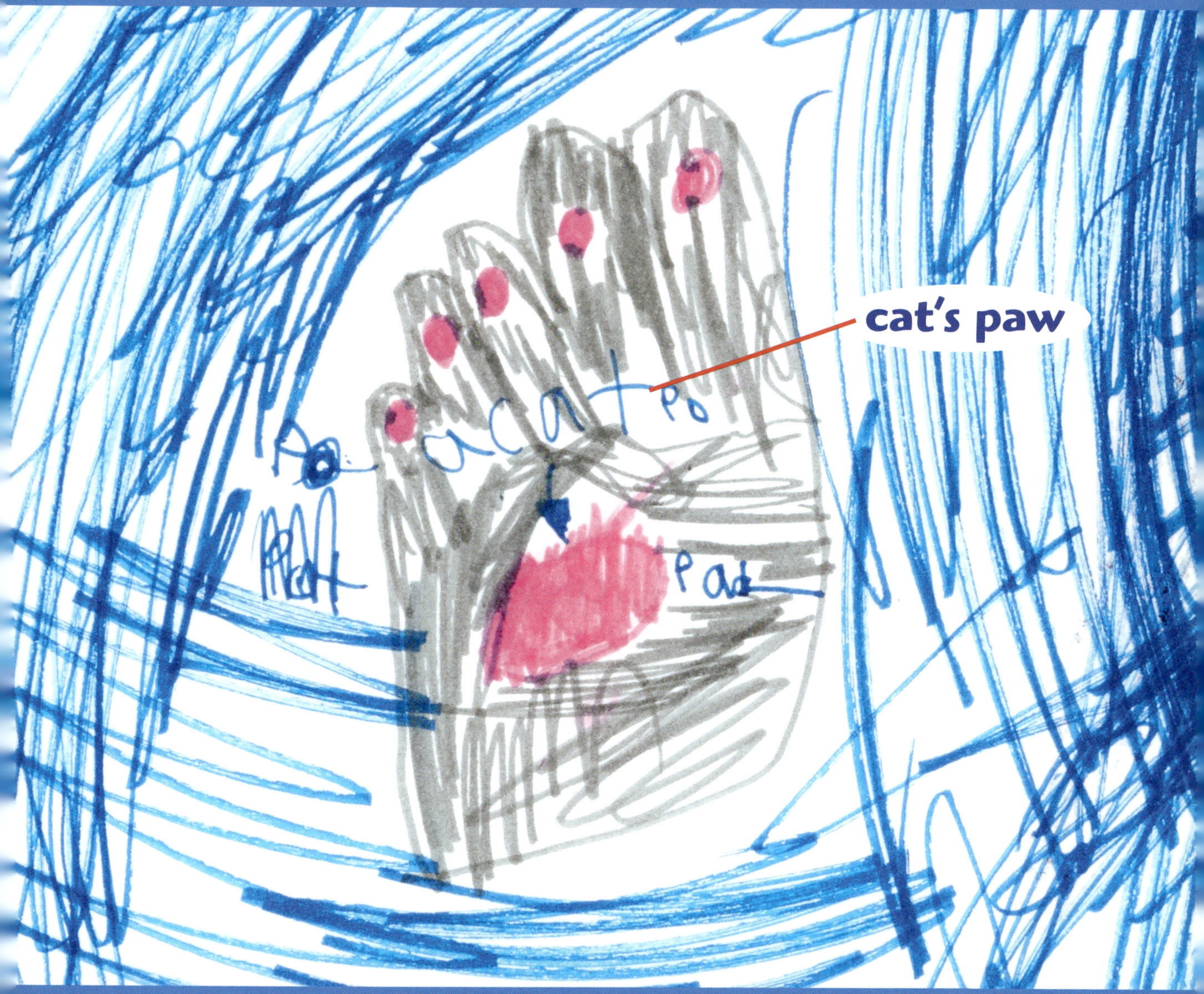
cat's paw

Cats

by Ella, Hayden, Kate, and Lili

Cats have sharp teeth and pads on their paws.

They use a scratching pole.

Wolves and Cats

by Aaron, Carter, Ella, Hayden, Kate, Nora, and Rowan

A cat lives in a house.

A wolf lives in a den.

Cat
WOlFS

A wolf is a wild animal.

A cat is a pet.

I don't think a wolf can raise a cat.